Bloom Where
You Are Planted

Bloom Where You Are Planted

Robert H. Schuller

HARVEST HOUSE PUBLISHERS
Eugene, Oregon 97402

BLOOM WHERE YOU ARE PLANTED

Copyright © 1978 by Robert H. Schuller
ISBN: 0-89081-154-7

CONTENTS

1

The Person Makes Success!

The place does not make the person; the person makes the place. That important life principle is based on one of my favorite verses in the Bible—Philippians 4:11. St. Paul writes:

"I have learned, in whatever state I am, to be content."

To put it in modern English, St. Paul is saying:

"I have learned how to be rich, how to be poor, how to be at comfort and how to take persecution. I have lived and walked with God, and I have learned that in whatever state of conditions or circumstances I find myself, I will not complain! I will make the best of it, confidently, and expect good things to come."

He practiced this principle! When he was thrown into prison, be bloomed where he was planted and produced what are now called the Prison Epistles.

Right now, you may be in a state of affairs, or in circumstances that you wish didn't exist. Well, just as you cannot tell a book by its cover, neither can you tell circumstances by their appearance.

I recently heard about a young man who was dashing through the airport to catch his plane. He was late, but as he passed the bookstore, he saw out of the corner of his eye a book entitled *How to Hug*. Being a very energetic young man, eager to win and influence his girlfriends, he quickly ran into the store, bought the book, eagerly anticipating reading it. Puffing passionately, he got on the airplane, opened his book on *How to Hug* and discovered he had purchased Volume 12 of an Encyclopedia! You just can't tell a book by its cover!

When I was growing up, I always thought that old women looked old, middle-aged women looked middle-aged, young girls looked young and little girls my age, well, they were just pretty and interesting. But today, times have really changed. You look at women today and they just don't show their age, and few of them really have had any face-lifting done. I don't know why this is, but it's really true.

I saw a woman not long ago who had to be about 80 years old, but she didn't look more than 50. I said to someone near me, "How old is she?" The fella said, "I don't know, but her Social Security number is four!"

You just can't tell a book by its cover. You just can't look at your situation or your circumstances and say, "I'm in a good spot," or "I'm in a bad spot." If you think that way, you're thinking wrong. *Every spot can be a good spot if God is in it!* It's that simple. It's not something you know by nature, it's something you have to learn. It's a mark of maturity.

This summer we flew in our travels to visit churches and mission stations. Our trip took us over the Tigris Euphrates Valley to the desert plains of Persia, and I was reminded of a story that came to me in full force with a renewed recollection when we were in Teheran.

The Crown Jewels of Persia are kept in Teheran in a very highly protected place, as are all the Crown Jewels of monarchs.

I have seen the Crown Jewels of England; they are in the Tower of London. I have seen the Crown Jewels of the Czar and Czarina of Russia; they are in the Hermitage Museum, in Leningrad. I have seen the Crown Jewels of many of the great kings of the centuries, but I have never in my life seen anything that comes close to the Crown Jewels of Persia. They defy description, and form, literally, the international banking collateral for that country.

Undoubtedly, the most beautiful crown ever fashioned for the head of a human being, is the crown that was designed for the present Princess of Iran—to be worn at her coronation. As I looked at the huge silver tray overflowing with diamonds, I whispered to our guide, "Where did all these diamonds come from?" He answered, "Many of them come from the marvelous Golcanda mine."

The Golcanda mine is where the Kohinoor diamond came from, which is in the Crown Jewels of England, and the Orloff diamond, which is in the Crown Jewels of Russia. The story of that mine was made famous in our country years ago by Russell Comwell's book, *Acres of Diamonds.*

Once there was a man named Ali Hafed, who lived in the beautiful country of Iran. He was a farmer, and was content in his state of affairs. His farm was good and fruitful. He had a wife and children and raised sheep, camels and wheat. "If a man has a wife, sons, camels, health and the peace of God," Ali Hafed often said, "He is rich!"

Ali Hafed was rich until one day a priest came to visit and began talking about a strange thing the priest called "diamonds." Ali Hafed had never heard of diamonds. The priest said, "They sparkle like a million suns. They are the most beautiful things in the world!"

Suddenly, Ali Hafed became very discontented with what he had. He asked the priest, "Where can you find these diamonds? I must have them." The priest answered, "They say they can be found all over the world. Look for a white stream that flows through white sands surrounded by high mountains, and you'll find diamonds.''

So Ali Hafed made a vow, sold his farm, left his wife and children in the care of a neighbor and set out on his journey to find diamonds.

He traveled through Palestine, then along the Nile Valley, until finally he found himself at the Pillars of Hercules, entering the country of Spain. He looked for white sands, tall mountains, but found no diamonds. With years passing, he came one day to the coast of Barcelona, Spain, broken, destitute and unable to communicate with his family. In a fit of despair and utter defeat, he plunged into the sea and died.

Meanwhile, the man who bought his farm spotted an odd black chunk of rock while watering his camel one day. He took the rock home, put it on his mantel and thought nothing more of it.

Stopping in one day, the priest looked at it and saw a flash of color from a crack in the rock. He said to the man, "A diamond! Where did you find it?"

The farmer said, "I found it by the cool sands and white stream where I water my camel."

Together, lifting their robes and running as fast as their sandaled feet would carry them, they rushed to the stream. They scratched and dug and found *more* diamonds! That discovery became the Golcanda Diamond Mine—the greatest diamond mine in the world!

The lesson is obvious. Diamonds were in Ali Hafed's own backyard all the time. But he didn't see them. Instead, he spent his lifetime in a fruitless search!

The moral is also obvious. You can spend your lifetime in all kinds of travels and pursuits of pleasure, fame and wealth—all in an effort to find happiness. But happiness can be found under your own feet, in your own backyard. Bloom where you are planted!

Wherever you are, God is. Wherever God is, there are beautiful plans—if only you will see the possibilities. God put you where you are because He can see diamonds in the rocks all around you.

2

The Person Makes Success!

If you were to list the names of the towns and cities wherein the greatest personalities in history have lived, I am sure most of you would list Rome, London, New York, Washington, Tokyo or Hong Kong. But the biggest people, on whom history hinged, did not live in those towns. Consider Cyrus the Great. Persepolis was his headquarters! Jesus of Nazareth—Bethlehem and Nazareth! Ghandi—the streets of India! Go on down the list of history, and what does it prove?

It proves that success and greatness does not depend on the place: *It depends on the person!* The place does not make the person; the person makes the place!

That's what is so exciting. Power, success and achievement will come to you anywhere you are if your attitude is right.

The lesson is this: It's not *where* you are, but *what* you are that matters. And that's why the people whose lives have blossomed most fragrantly in human history often appear to have set up their headquarters in obscure cities, and the cities have become famous because they were there.

How do you bloom where you are planted? By thinking of the possibilities! Look at the possibilities under your feet right now, whatever your situation.

Not long ago I read about an elderly man who was known in his lifetime to be very rich because he was so thrifty—almost to the point of being considered a miser. When he died, it was discovered that in his room he had gallon cans filled with nickels. The bank examiner reported that the man saved most of his money and used it to put young needy men through college. That was why he was so thrifty! "That explains why he always looked so happy and contented," his neighbors remarked. It was also discovered that after he retired, each day he would fill his pockets with nickels and make it a ritual to walk down the streets of the business districts looking for cars whose parking meters had expired. When he found one, he would drop in a nickel! Now there was a happy man.

Bloom where you are planted. There are acres of diamonds under your feet right now—diamonds of joy, happiness and purposefulness in life. All you need to discover them is a dynamic, positive attitude.

Here in California we have many Army bases, and during the Second World War many of our young men were trained on them. One of these bases is located in a bleak, remote section of the desert.

There is a story of one young soldier who brought his wife out with him to this desert outpost. They wanted to be together as much as possible before he went overseas. The only housing they could find was an old shack that had been abandoned by the Indians.

For the first few days, the wife found it tolerable, and even rather pleasant. She and her new husband were together. But days added to days and the hours became long, lonely and boring. Then the winds came, the sand storms struck and the heat went up over 115°. To her, the situation became intolerable!

When her husband was assigned to spend two weeks deeper in the desert, she reached the bottom of her negative, lonely attitude. She wrote her mother, saying:

"Mother,
I'm coming home. I can't
stand it here."

Within a week, she received a letter back from her mother with only these lines:

"Dear Daughter,
Two men sit in prison bars.
One sees mud, the other stars.
Love,
Mother"

She read the lines over and over again, until she became ashamed of herself. That night she thought, "I wonder what the stars look like from here." She went out of her shack and discovered what many Californians know—in no other place in the world do the stars shine brighter than over the deserts of California. She thrilled to the beauty of the stars.

The next day she decided to take a walk, to explore her community. She walked down the road to the Indians who lived in shacks not far from her. They had never spoken, and she was certain the Indians were hostile and unfriendly. But she began talking to two women who were weaving. When the Indian women saw the woman was friendly, they became friendly. When she stopped *thinking* they were hostile, they stopped *being* hostile. Before she knew it, she was learning how to weave baskets.

One day several little Indian boys brought her seashells and told her the legend of how long ago the desert was the ocean floor. She became intrigued and started to collect sea shells in the desert. She was fascinated!

By the time her husband finished his assignment at that base, she had become such an authority on the desert that she had written a book on it! She fell in love with the desert and wept when she had to say good-bye to the most beautiful friends she had ever had—the Indians.

Bloom where you are planted. I have learned that in whatever circumstance, condition or place I find myself, with the help of God, I can turn it into a garden. It's possible, if you keep a happy, positive attitude. You will begin to bloom when you exercise a deep beautiful faith that God didn't make a mistake when he put you where you are!

I want to share with you one of the most beautiful letters I have ever received:

"Dear Dr. Schuller,

Three years ago, I admitted myself to Bethesda Mental Hospital in Denver, Colorado, for two and a half weeks. It

was the most beautiful experience of
my life. I thank God for it. When I was
there I wrote these lines, and I want to
share them with you. I'm not a poet,
and the rhyming may not be right, but it
comes from my heart.

"I walked through the doors;
They slammed shut behind me.
There was nothing but sadness
and gloom.
My mind was a blank, I didn't
give a—
But there was nothing else I
could do.
They put me in a room with two
other women;
We stared at each other and
glared.
They were blue, depressed and
numb just as I
But mostly plain scared.

"What would happen to us? Did
anybody care?
Why are we here, in this room
bleak and bare?
Please God, what will happen
to us.

There were people there from
all walks of life;
A preacher, a teacher, a Col-
onel, a racer,
a salesman, secretary, house-
wife, baker.
But the saddest of all were the
young folks on dope.
For them I saw not a glimmer of
hope.

"The thing that made such an
impression on me,
Was something I heard, it was
almost a plea:

Walk tall, my friend, walk tall.
No matter how down and out
you may be,
No matter what fate has in store
for thee,
You've got to be true to your-
self, my friend,
Before you walk out that door.

"Oh yes, I was in a mental hos-
pital, my friends,
But things are looking up instead
of down.
My head's in the air, not down
on my chest;
A smile has replaced the frown.
It was hell, it was heaven, all
rolled into one.
Let me be the first one to say,
I thank God on my knees today.
He gave me the privilege to send
me that way.

"When you're so discouraged,
And life's a bad scene.
When suicide seems the only
way out,
Look, breathe deep, God won't
let you fall.
Just remember the words, walk
tall, walk tall!"

Wherever you are today, there are great possibilities. There are diamonds under your feet, believe me. Your life can bloom wherever you are if you will think positive and try positively to help someone around you. Get interested in someone else who's hurting.

There was a ship that had sailed from the Orient coming up around the coast of South America. It had been a long voyage and the territory was new to the captain and his crew. They misjudged their water supply, and soon, off the coast of

South America, they ran out. The entire crew was threatened with death from lack of water.

Fortunately, a passing ship flying a South American flag came by, and the distressed vessel signaled, "Can you share your water?" The passing ship signaled back, "Dip where you are."

The distressed captain thought it was an insane command and repeated his request. Again, the signal came back, "Dip where you are."

So a bucket and rope were lowered and the captain dipped into the salty ocean, lifted up a bucket of water, put his fingers in it, touched his tongue and found the water was sweet. What he did not know was they were in the center of a mile-wide current in the ocean where the Amazon River was still making its surging inrush into the ocean!

Learn that whatever state you find yourself, there are diamonds waiting to be mined. God put you where you are, and this week you're going to have a wonderful time living as you practice this faith!

3

Opportunities Under Your Feet

I want to turn your attention to a Bible verse that, in a subtle way, really has a lot of inspiration in it. In writing to the church in Philippi, St. Paul adds in a closing verse this simple sentence:

> *"All the saints greet you, especially, those of Caesar's household"* (Philippians 4:22).

Isn't that amazing? Even with all its visciousness, immorality and crime, there were Christians in the palace of Caesar!

How can you be a Christian in today's world? How can you be faithful to God Monday through Friday? *It's possible!* It's possible for people to be Christians to the point where St. Paul thought of them as *saints* in that unlikely place: *Caesar's household!* It's like saying that committed Christians have infiltrated the core of Communist cells in Eastern Europe! It's possible, for God has a way of scattering seeds so that they will bloom in the most unlikely places.

Bloom where you are planted. Your attitude—more than anything else—will determine whether you are a success or a failure.

J. W. Moran tells a story about visiting a friend and discovering some beautiful flowers pressed in his friend's old Bible. He neither knew the name nor the description of them, so he asked his friend who said, "These flowers were discovered on an expedition up a lonely, rocky promontory on the coast of New Zealand. My wife and I were exploring the region when we came across this terribly rocky stretch that probed out into the ocean. There, in the most unlikely collection of rocks, was this profusion of blooming wild flowers. What they were and where they came from we did not know; we were mystified to see them blooming in such an unlikely place! Evidently a seed blew in from a passing steamer, and it found its way into that little crevice, because the flowers are found in no other place in New Zealand. We were so inspired that we cut them, brought them home and pressed them.

Flowers in a rocky promontory! Saints in Caesar's household. Bloom where you are planted. Chances are, right under your feet, wherever you are, there is a beautiful opportunity—now!

I am reminded of an experience I had while visiting New Zealand last summer. I was told that one of the wonders of the world is the existence of the caves in

Waitomo, one hundred miles north of Auckland, New Zealand. Once, they tell me, there was a farmer who owned the place, then sold it, now knowing that right under his land was one of the eight most beautiful wonders of the world!

In no place in the whole world can you see caves like you see here. You make your way down into the earth, walking the damp, dark hallway, holding onto an iron rail until you come to what is an underground river. Here you are told to get into a little boat and "not to utter a sound." You float down this underground stream, through underground caverns, to see a sight of amazing beauty. The guide who handles the little boat does not want to disturb the source of the living colors you are about to see, so he does not even paddle the boat. He quietly places his hands along the side of the damp canyon underground and nudges the boat slowly through the thick, inky darkness. The blackness is *solid*, total!

Suddenly you spot a billion sparkling little lights. For a moment you think you are in the desert on a clear night and seeing the Milky Way right above you! (You have lost all sense of perspective there in the dark tunnel!) The lights are really only four feet above your head! And what you see are the glowing lights of millions of glowworms that live in the caves! Twinkling, glowing like a million little neon lights, you can now hear—if you are very still—the chorus of the buzzing of these beautiful creatures.

Once God said to Moses, "Moses, what is in your hand?" Moses answered, "A rod." God must have smiled and said, "Ah, but don't underestimate that rod."

What's under *your* feet? What's in *your* hand? I want to give you four very simple but very workable tips that will help you to bloom where you are. I believe you can be a flower in a craggy wall or a saint in Caesar's household. I believe you can be a positive thinker in a world of negative thinkers or a shining light for Jesus Christ in a colony of people who despise you.

1. *Think positively.*

To bloom where you are planted may test your positive thinking to the limit. But do try to *think positively constantly.* Remember this principle: There's a *purpose for every place and every person under the sun. God has a purpose for every person in every place.*

Let me give you a short, simple sentence that will help you:

GOD HAS NO WASTEBASKETS

God doesn't believe in waste! There's nothing that, in His mind, has to be thrown away as worthless!

I recently read a story in a hotel room in Tokyo.

"There was a Chinese wife who said to her husband, 'I would like a new coat.' Her husband said to her, 'What will you do with your old coat?' She answered, 'I will make a bed cover out of it.' He said, 'What will you do with your old bed cover?' She replied, 'I will make pillowcases out of it.' He asked, 'What will you do with the old pillowcases?' She responded, 'I will make new cleaning cloths' He said, 'What will you do with the old cleaning cloths?' She said, 'I will tie them together and make a mop out of them.' He continued, 'What will you do with the old mop?' She said, 'I will chop it up into little pieces, mix it with cement, and in the springtime we will patch the holes in our cottage.' He said, 'All right. You may have a new coat!' " If an Oriental can find a good purpose and use to every-thing—what can God do?

Dr. Henry Poppen, who spent forty years in China, once said to me, "We didn't throw away anything in China. We *even used ashes!*" I discovered this during my trip to Korea. In Korea they use ashes to fill the pockholes in the streets! *Nothing is wasted.* (more than one American has been embarassed after travelling through the Orient to find that when he gets home after a period of time, he gets a gift from the hotel operator. In the package are all the little things he threw in his wastebasket!)

God has no wastebaskets. He has a purpose for every place and every per-son under the sun. Think positively and start to bloom where you are.

2. *Believe the best about every situa-tion.*

Look for the best in every place, and

believe the best about every person around you. Negative thinkers believe the worst about the place, the person and the situation.

I read the other day about a very distinguished businessman on the Long Island commuter train going into New York City. An unshaven man in a shabby coat brushed close to him, bumped him in the chest and made his way to the door about to get off at the next stop. As an afterthought the businessman felt his pocket and discovered that his wallet was gone. Just then the train stopped, the doors opened, and the businessman grabbed the shoulders of the fellow who had bumped into him. Captured, the grubby fellow turned around with a horrified, frightened and desperate look on his face. Suddenly he lunged forward, broke free from his coat, and jumped off the train! The doors closed! And the businessman was left holding the culprit's coat! Immediately he went through the pockets, expecting to find his wallet, but they were empty! He went on to his office where his wife called him later in the morning and said, "Oh, honey, you left your wallet on the dresser this morning." (No wonder that poor unshaven fellow was so scared when he was getting off the train! He thought someone was robbing or attacking *him!*)

That's how wars and divorces start, and that's how problems in corporations begin. Someone jumps to a negative conclusion, thinking the worst about someone else! The most dangerous person in the world is a negative thinker who puts two and two together. Believe the *best* about someone. Think positively! Believe the best about persons, positions and situations.

3. Now, *remember always to be a positive reactionary.*

It's not what happens to you but how you react to it that determines whether you will bloom where you are, or dry up and die where you are.

There was a man who was striken with an illness that left him totally paralyzed. A friend who hadn't seem him for many years came to his bedside and was struck by the change in his countenance and personality that followed this lengthy illness. Looking at his beautiful face as he was resting in bed, the friend said, "Sickness and trouble really colors a personality, doesn't it?" The paralyzed man replied, "Yes, it does, and I decided that I would choose the colors and make them beautiful."

When you have a positive idea, *react positively!* A fear of failure could tempt you to react negatively. Don't allow the fear of faiure to dominate your thinking. Here's how you can conquer it. You simply say, "I've got an idea. I think it may be a God-given idea. I don't know if it will be a successful or a non-successful idea, so I will become a researcher and an experimenter. I will try it. If I try it and it works—great! If I try it and my idea doesn't prove successful, I will have been a successful researcher! I will have found out what didn't work. *Researchers never fail!*

4. Now *tackle your problems positively and creatively.*

You can follow steps one, two and three and still run into problems. Of course, problems can cause you to shrivel up instead of blossoming in success. The important thing to remember is: *every problem can be solved!* If you run across what seems to be an unsolvable problem, chances are you have not properly *iden-*

tified it. The hardest part of solving problems is to correctly identify them.

There is a leading automobile manufacturer in Detroit, Michigan, that has this letter on file:

"Dear Sirs:

I have one of your new cars, and I have a complaint about it. My complaint is that the car runs fine, until I go out and buy vanilla ice cream. I know you may think I'm crazy, but I'm serious! I buy my family ice cream every night. If I buy strawberry, chocolate or nut ice cream, my car starts fine! But if I buy vanilla ice cream the thing won't start!"

The top echelon in this automobile company laughed about this letter. Then someone said, "I don't think we should laugh. Let's send one of our engineers out there to check it out."

So an engineer went out and got a

motel room near this man's home. He went to the man's house, found that he was a college graduate and that he lived in a fine part of his community. Every night the man would say to his family, "What kind of ice cream shall I buy tonight?" The kids would make their choice, and he would go out and buy the ice cream flavor they wanted. True enough, the car started fine, except when the man bought vanilla ice cream. The engineer went along every night for over two weeks until he finally figured out the problem.

In this particular ice cream shop all the flavored ice cream was at the end of the store, while the vanilla ice cream was right at the entrance door. There was always a line of people waiting to buy the flavored ice cream, and never a lineup for vanilla. So when he bought vanilla ice cream, he was only in the store a couple of minutes—and when he bought flavored ice cream he was in the store ten minutes! The problem was not the flavor of ice cream—the problem was *time!* Now the case could be responsibly diagnosed!

The problem with the car was a vapor lock. The car vapor-locked every night, but the extra five or ten minute wait for the flavored ice cream was enough time for the vapor lock to disappear. When the engineer diagnosed the problem right, he was able to solve it. The hardest part of solving problems is to correctly identify them.

Here is the point. Some of you think your problem is, "I'm living in the wrong community." "I belong to the wrong company." "I'm married to the wrong man." "I'm married to the wrong woman." *I will tell you that in nine hundred and ninety-nine cases out of a thousand* you haven't correctly identified the problem. The real problem is *your attitude!* Your *negative* attitude!

Think positively, try positively, and tackle your problems positively and creatively.

Trust God confidently. You didn't ask to be born. Chances are you had nothing to say about your parentage, the color of your skin, your national origin, probably not even the fact you are living where you are.

But God has been guiding you. He has a plan for you. Philippians 1:6 says:

> *"And I am sure that He who began a good work in you will bring it to completion at the day of Jesus Christ."*

Dare to believe that you can blossom for Jesus Christ—right where you are! *Trust God confidently!*

Someone with a problem is going to touch your life soon; someone with a problem that only Jesus Christ can heal, that only Christ can satisfy. *You* be the saint in Caesar's household. *You* begin to bloom where you are planted! God will use you if you will think and try positively.

Instead of tossing ideas and dreams into the wastebasket, *throw the wastebasket away and replace it with a tackle box.* Then *tackle* every problem prayerfully, trusting in God.

You can be confident that God wants every flower to bloom. He wants every seed to sprout. He wants every person to experience joy and peace! That includes *YOU!* Bloom where you are planted!

NOTES